Myths and Civilization of the

ANCIENT
MESOPOTAMIANS

Copyright © 2001 by McRae Books, Florence, Italy

This edition published in 2002 by
Peter Bedrick Books, an imprint of
McGraw-Hill Children's Publishing
8787 Orion Place
Columbus, OH 43240
www.MHkids.com

ISBN 0-87226-593-5
CIP information is on file with
McGraw-Hill Children's Publishing.

The Myths & Civilization series
was created and produced by McRae Books,
via de' Rustici, 5 – Florence, Italy
e-mail info@mcraebooks.com

Editor Susan Kelly
Illustrations Francesca D'Ottavi (myths), Ivan Stalio, Alessandro Cantucci,
Andrea Morandi, Daniela Astone (civilization)
Graphic Design Marco Nardi
Layout and Cutouts Laura Ottina, Adriano Nardi
Color separations Litocolor, Florence (Italy)

Printed and bound in Italy by Nuova G.E.P.

04 03 02   1   2   3   4
First edition

**McGraw-Hill
Children's Publishing**
A Division of The McGraw-Hill Companies

Myths and Civilization of the
ANCIENT MESOPOTAMIANS

Rupert Matthews

Illustrations by
Francesca D'Ottavi
Studio Stalio
(Alessandro Cantucci, Andrea Morandi)

PETER BEDRICK BOOKS

CONTENTS

INTRODUCTION

The ancient lands of Mesopotamia are unfamiliar territory for many people. Yet they were home to the earliest civilization in the world. It was here that the first farmers learned to cultivate grain, growing what they needed rather than gathering wild varieties. They also tamed sheep and goats, keeping them for their meat, hides, and wool. The world's first cities grew up in Mesopotamia, and many of its earliest empires also flourished here. The peoples of Mesopotamia, who were among the first to use the written word, have left us many myths and legends. In this book, we have tried to associate the myths with the historical context in which they were created so that we can better understand them both.

HOW THIS BOOK WORKS

This book is divided into sections. Each one begins with a myth, strikingly illustrated on a black background. This is followed by a nonfiction spread with information about Mesopotamian society.

Spread with a myth about the hero Gilgamesh's quest to find the secret of eternal life is followed by one about religion.

The Mesopotamians left behind a large number of written records carved into clay tablets. They record many different things, from sheep counts for taxation purposes, to religious practises and myths and legends. Even though many of the stories are incomplete, or have been pieced together over the years from different versions, they still help us to come surprisingly close to a people that existed so long ago. The stories in our book are based on myths that were forgotton at about the time Christ died. Archeologists learned how to read them again about 150 years ago when they deciphered Akkadian, one of the area's ancient tongues.

MARDUK AND THE BABYLONIAN CREATION MYTH

At the very beginning of time, the two great gods Apsu and Tiamat existed alone. They created creatures to serve them – dragons and giant scorpions, fish-men and blood-drinking rams – and they created other gods as well. But soon these other gods began to annoy Apsu with their noisy talking and singing. He wanted to destroy them.

Ea, god of the rivers, learned of Apsu's decision. He called a meeting to warn the other gods and goddesses. None of them knew what to do, but Ea devised a plan and destroyed Apsu. Tiamat was furious and wanted revenge for Apsu's death, so she created an army of fearsome monsters. Both Ea and his father Anshar went forward in turn to do battle with Tiamat, but both were defeated. Then Marduk, son of Ea, spoke up. "I have a plan to defeat the monster Tiamat," he said. "But if I risk my life to save you, and succeed, I want you to make me king of you all." The other gods agreed.

Marduk prepared weapons of flames, lightning, winds, floods, and storms. When he challenged Tiamat to battle, she opened her mouth to tear at him, but before she could do any harm, Marduk released the winds. Tiamat tried to swallow them, but the winds filled up her whole body so that she could not close her mouth. Then Marduk shot an arrow into her stomach, which split her body open and pierced her heart. Marduk threw Tiamat to the ground and tore her body in half. One half he made into the Earth and the other half became the sky. Marduk formed the sky with stars, moon, and sun, and he set the length of the days, months, and years. Then he shaped the land into mountains, valleys, and hills. From Tiamat's eyes he made the Euphrates and Tigris Rivers. In the most fertile valley he created a place he would make his own. He called it Babylon.

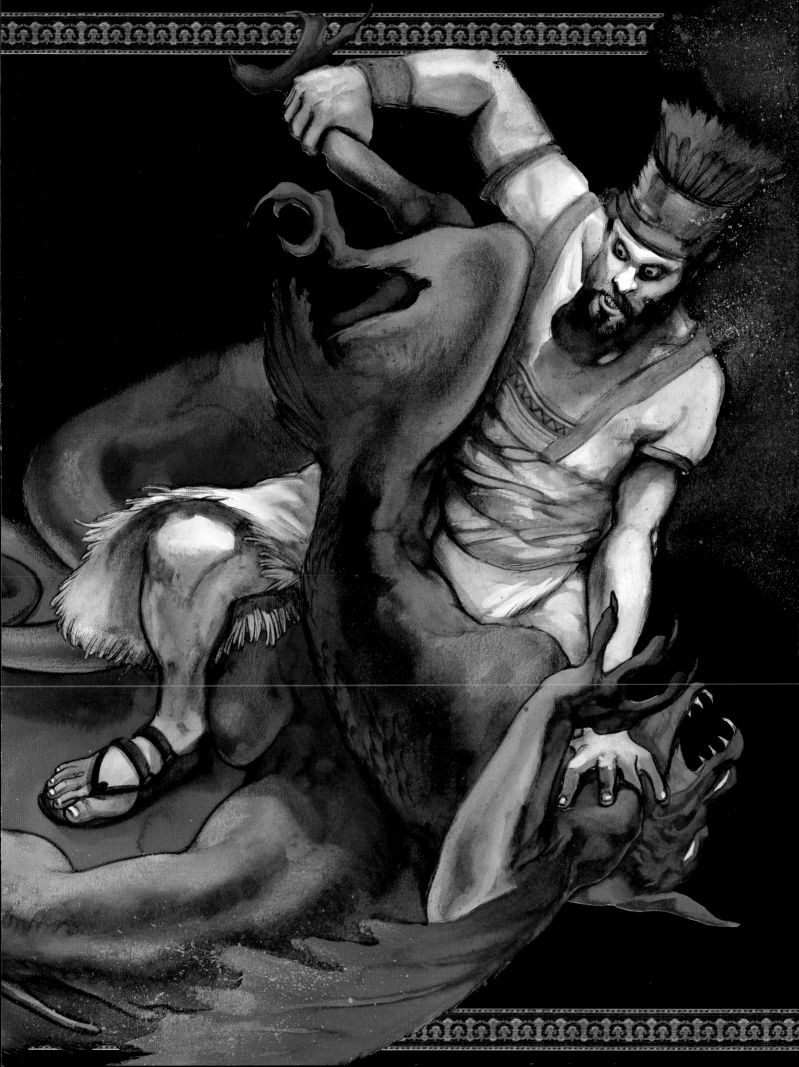

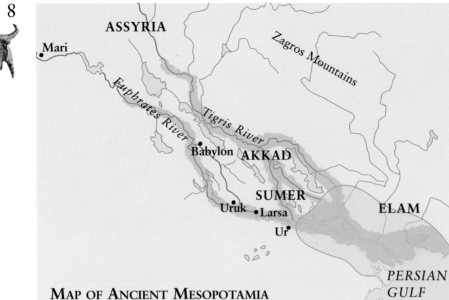

ASSYRIA

Mari

Zagros Mountains

Euphrates River

Tigris River

Babylon AKKAD

SUMER

Uruk • Larsa

Ur

ELAM

PERSIAN
GULF

MAP OF ANCIENT MESOPOTAMIA

The Face of Mesopotamia

The heartland of the early civilization was in Sumer, where the first cities were built, though society was first organized under kings in Kish. The center of power in Mesopotamia moved between Sumer and Babylonia, and, several times, even further north to Assyria. The peoples of Elam never settled into cities, though they adopted many Sumerian ways of life. And the Zagros Mountains were home to tough nomadic tribes who raided the fertile valleys and attacked the cities, as did the nomads of Arabia to the south.

This map shows ancient Mesopotamia. The courses of the Tigris and the Euphrates Rivers changed several times over the years and there is some evidence that the Persian Gulf may have flooded deep into Elam at times.

Below: Longhorn sheep decorate this stone bowl from the 4th millennium BC. Sheep in some areas of the Near East still look very similar to this today.

Above: A domestic goat, like those herded by the earliest people to live in Mesopotamia. Some people still keep goats like this today.

CHRONOLOGY OF ANCIENT MESOPOTAMIA

	Towns and temples appear in Mesopotamia *c. 5000 BC*	Reign of Sargon the Great 2334–2279 BC	Old Assyrian Period *c. 1800–1700 BC*	Babylon occupied by Assyrians 729 BC	Fall of Babylon, Beginning of Persian Dominance 539 BC
Irrigation and agricultural settlements in southern Mesopotamia *c. 5500 BC*	First cities appear in southern Mesopotamia *c. 3500 BC*	First Dynasty of Babylon 1894–1595 BC	Assyria regains independence 1400	Fall of Assyrian Empire 612 BC	Persian Empire at its Peak 521–486 BC

The Origins of Mesopotamian Civilization

Ancient Mesopotamia was a rich and fertile country that occupied the long valley that the Tigris and Euphrates Rivers flow through. The word "Mesopotamia" originally meant "between the rivers." It was here that the earliest cities developed, each one dominating an area of farmland. As time passed, kings or priests started to rule the cities. Some conquered others and built up mighty empires. The culture and civilization that developed in Mesopotamia influenced the later civilizations of Egypt, Greece, and Rome. Even today, the influence of the ancient Mesopotamians can still be seen. Like them, we count time in twelves, and have seven days in a week.

This tiny pottery model boat was made in Eridu around 4000 BC. The boat is almost identical to those still used by fishermen in southern Iraq.

Left: Made about 5200 BC, this jug is painted with a face on its neck. The use of such fragile objects indicates that the owners inhabited settled villages, rather than living as nomads.

Wild einkorn

Wild emmer

The birth of farming

Early humans survived by hunting animals and gathering wild plants. However, about 10,000 years ago, people abandoned this lifestyle and began growing their own plants and breeding animals. They became farmers. This change began in the Middle East where bands of nomadic humans herded wild goats together as a ready source of milk and meat. Wild grains – such as emmer and einkorn, which are types of wheat – grew in the hills west of Mesopotamia. To begin with, people simply collected these grains from the wild, but by 7000 BC some villages relied on fields of planted wheat that the people grew and harvested.

Right: The wild ancestors of modern grains have smaller seeds and brittle stems.

Right: Bread was a staple food. To make bread, grains were ground by hand using stone pestles and mortars. The resulting flour was then mixed with water, and baked in an oven.

GILGAMESH AND THE SECRET OF ETERNAL LIFE

After the death of his great friend Enkidu, the hero Gilgamesh of Uruk mourned deeply and began to fear his own death. Filled with grief, he roamed the countryside and set out to find the home of Utanapishtim, who was the only human to know the secret of eternal life. After surviving many dangers on his travels, Gilgamesh found Utanapishtim and asked him to share the secret of his immortality. Utanapishtim told Gilgamesh that, unlike some of the gods and spirits, all humans must die eventually. However, old men could become young again by eating a special plant of rejuvenation, which grew in the depths of the ocean. Utanapishtim warned that the plant was so covered in thorns that anyone who touched it would be cut badly.

Gilgamesh at once rowed out into the ocean in a boat, tied heavy stones to his feet, and leapt into the water. The stones dragged Gilgamesh to the bottom of the ocean where he saw the spiky plant. Gilgamesh grabbed the plant and suffered deep scratches, but he cut himself free from the stones and rose to the water's surface with the plant. He swam ashore and set out on his journey to carry the wonderful plant all the way home to Uruk.

On the way, Gilgamesh came across a spring of pure water. He stopped to bathe his bleeding hands. As he washed, a snake slithered out from the pool, snatched up the sweet-smelling plant in its strong mouth, and raced away with it.

Gilgamesh sat down and wept for his loss. "Was it for this that I toiled with my hands? Is it for this that I have wrung out my heart's blood? For myself I have gained nothing; not I, but the beast has joy of it now. I will leave this place and go." Sadly, Gilgamesh finally understood that he was not meant to be immortal. He returned home to Uruk, and when the city came into view, he saw the towering walls that he had built around the city. He realized that, even though he was destined to die as all people do, others would remember him for a very long time as the man who had created a magnificent city.

Resigned at last to his own mortality, the wise Gilgamesh continued to rule Uruk until death came to take him to join his friend Enkidu.

Religion

Mesopotamian religion featured many demons, mythological animals, and spirits, as well as gods and goddesses. Every human activity – such as war, growing crops, hunting, or sleeping – had its own particular god or spirit, as did natural events such as day and night, rain, or floods. It was very important to perform the correct rituals when worshiping the deities, so they would not become angry and punish the people. Ceremonies were held, and food was regularly offered. On special days, statues of particular deities were taken out of their temples and carried around in processions for all the people to see.

Left: An eagle-headed minor god sprinkles water using a pine cone. These spirits were considered friendly to humans.

Right: The winged demon Pazuzu could bring scorching winds from the desert to shrivel crops.

Mythological creatures
Mesopotamian myths are filled with magical or supernatural beasts. Seven evil monsters were thought to live in the western mountains and to breathe out disease. A lion-headed eagle was believed to fly among the clouds and create rain.

Left: A Babylonian stone marker, sacred to the god Marduk.

Right: This Sumerian panel shows a donkey playing a lyre for a bear, from a scene described in a now-lost animal myth.

Prayers and priests

All the gods and goddesses had temples, and priests or priestesses took care of formal worship and regular offerings of food to the deity. This ensured that the city would continue to enjoy the favor of the god. A person who wanted to be blessed by a god, or to have a curse removed, would go to the temple and perform a ceremony such as peeling an onion on the altar or burning a mat on the floor. Priests presided over the ceremonies and often charged the visitor.

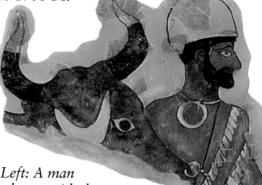

Below: A bull being taken to be sacrificed to the gods in Mari about 1700 BC.

Left: A man shown with the wide eyes and clasped hands of a devout worshiper. This small statue was found in the Temple of Abu in Eshnunna and was made about 2700 BC.

Above: This statue of a priestess wearing a ceremonial cloak is from about 2400 BC.

Sacrifices and rituals

Mesopotamians believed in dozens of demons and spirits. The demon Lamashu, for instance, attacked babies at birth. Only specific rituals could guard against these demons, or attract friendly spirits. These ceremonies sometimes involved sacrificing an animal or valuable object. Human sacrifice was rare and was only practiced by kings.

Left: This reconstruction shows the ziggurat of Babylon, which was dedicated to the god Marduk.

Right: A war god stabs a sun god. This decoration on a baked earth tablet may have been an illustration of a now-lost myth.

Below: This carving shows the sun god Shamash sitting on a throne and being visited by a king and two other gods. The symbol in the center represents the sun.

Gods and temples

The temple of the chief god in each city was built as a ziggurat. These massive tower-platforms were built of mud brick and were topped by small temples which only the priests and kings could enter. Mud brick is a weak material, so the ziggurats had to be rebuilt every 100 years or so.

Utanapishtim Survives the Great Flood

In the distant past, the great god Enlil, lord of the air, became very angry. He called together Anu, his father, Ninurta, his servant, and Ennugi, the god of canals. Enlil told them, "The uproar of mankind is intolerable and sleep is impossible." The other gods agreed, and they decided to destroy mankind. They sent for Adad, god of storms, and told him to create a mighty storm that would flood the entire Earth with water.

But the plot was overheard by Ea, god of the rivers that nourish mankind. He believed some humans should survive, and so he warned his favorite human, whose name was Utanapishtim of Shurrupak. He told Utanapishtim to build a large ship with seven decks and to load it with all his wealth, his family and servants, as well as seeds and pairs of every kind of animal.

Utanapishtim did as he was told, and finished building the ship in just seven days. On the evening of the seventh day, Adad flew down from the hills and created a great storm. Heavy rain battered the land for six days and seven nights, and after this the entire Earth was flooded. By the seventh day, the storm had exhausted itself. The winds died down, and the waters quieted and began to recede. Utanapishtim released first a dove and then a swallow from the boat, but both came back. Finally he let a raven out, and when it did not return he knew that the bird had found somewhere to land.

Then Ishtar, the goddess of love, came to Earth and cried, "Alas, the days of old are turned to dust. Are these not my people?" The tip of a mountain then appeared from beneath the waters and Utanapishtim ran his ship onto the dry ground. After seven days, the flood waters receded. Utanapishtim opened the four doors of his ship and let all of the people and animals out.

Enlil was furious that any people had survived the flood. He came down to kill Utanapishtim, but Ea and Ishtar stopped him. Instead, Utanapishtim was taken away by the gods to live in a beautiful house where the rivers run into the sea. He and his wife were made immortal and given an endless supply of food.

Gods and Goddesses

The ancient Mesopotamians believed in dozens of different gods and goddesses. Kings were often thought to be appointed by, or descended from, the gods. Each city had its own patron god or goddess, who the people considered to be more important than the other gods. To add to the confusion, the same god could be known by different names in different cities. Eventually, the priests of Babylon started to organize a hierarchy of the gods. It is this late arrangement of earlier myths and stories that has survived until today.

Above: A goddess of animals and vegetation, from about 1250 BC. She is dressed in Minoan style, indicating that she may originate from Greek lands.

Left: The goddess Ishtar shown on a silver dish from about AD 300, sitting on her sacred lion and holding symbols of the sun and moon.

The Pantheon

The gods and goddesses of Mesopotamia were believed to live in their own carefully structured society. Each divinity, or divine family, had its own palace, complete with servants and soldiers. These palaces were thought to float above the sky or to lie beneath the Earth's surface. There was also a great hall called Upshukina, where the gods would gather to discuss the fates of humans and other matters. Temples dedicated to different gods and goddesses were thought of as their houses in the human world.

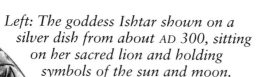

ANIMALS IN MESOPOTAMIAN RELIGION

The Mesopotamians had no animal gods, but several deities were associated with animals that were considered sacred. Ishtar, for example, is often shown riding a lion. Spirits were often shown as animals, such as the eagle-headed spirit that watched over mankind from above, or the bull-spirit (left) that used its great strength to drive evil spirits away from the king.

Above: A symbolic battle between the serpent of knowledge and the lion of Ishtar, on a pottery vessel from about 2700 BC.

Sacrifices

The Mesopotamians frequently sacrificed animals or crops to the gods. One poem records the gratitude of the gods for an offering of roast meat: "The gods smelled the good odor, they swarmed like flies above him who offered them sacrifice." It was believed that regular sacrifices would keep the gods happy and stop them from spreading disease, famine, or destruction on Earth.

Above: A king dressed as the Babylonian god Marduk carries a lamb to be sacrificed.

Above: A small figure of a calf. Religious offerings like this were symbolic reminders of live animal sacrifices made to the gods.

Right: This group of three sacred rams with gilded faces was found in Larsa and is from about 1750 BC.

Gods in art

Babylonians represented their gods as statues, carvings, or paintings. Different deities can be recognized by the symbols that they carry and by their different characteristics.

Left: This human-headed bull symbolized the divine power that the gods gave to kings.

Below: Lilit, a Babylonian-Assyrian goddess, in her sacred cloak.

Below: Nergal, god of the Underworld, with his serpents.

Above: A figure of Ishtar, emphasizing her role as a fertility goddess.

Above: The storm god, Adad, holding bolts of lightning and a hammer of thunder.

Above: A minor god with four wings, carrying a pine cone, able to drive away evil demons.

THE MARRIAGE OF ISHTAR AND TAMMUZ

Ishtar, the goddess of love, traveled the Earth looking for a husband. One day she came across two men. One was named Tammuz, and he was the shepherd of the gods. The other was named Enkimbu, and he was the farmer of the gods.

Enkimbu was a strong man who looked after wide fields of beautiful grain and other crops. He had great wealth and had much to offer a wife. But Ishtar fell in love with Tammuz. Tammuz was tall and muscular, and he was the most handsome man that Ishtar had ever seen. Although he was poor, Tammuz was so good-looking that Ishtar chose him at once to be her husband.

After they were married Ishtar took Tammuz to her palace in the sky where they could live together and enjoy each other's love far away from the interruptions of gods or men. For many years all was well, but then Tammuz began to grow bored.

"You travel the Earth giving the gift of love to people and animals," he complained to his wife. "But I stay here and grow miserable without you. I need something to do."

Ishtar asked her husband what he wanted to do. Tammuz replied that when he had been a shepherd he had enjoyed hunting wild boar. "Allow me to go back to Earth to hunt boar while you are away," he begged. Ishtar refused.

"Why can you not be happy here where you are safe and away from the cares of the world?" she asked. But Tammuz continued to beg.

At last, Ishtar gave in. She gave Tammuz a spear and showed him how to return to Earth when she was absent. Tammuz enjoyed himself hunting on many occasions. Then, one day, he missed a boar with his spear. The enraged boar turned on Tammuz, threw him to the ground and ripped open his stomach with his tusks.

When Ishtar came home that day, Tammuz was missing. Ishtar searched for Tammuz and found him lying dead. Ishtar burst out weeping and cried, "Tammuz, Tammuz, I have killed you. Tammuz, Tammuz, you are no more." Ishtar was heartbroken and determined to bring her husband back from the dead. She set out for the Underworld.

Food and Agriculture

The basis of all the power and wealth of Mesopotamia was the food produced by farming in the region. The fertile fields, irrigated by waters from the twin rivers, produced far more food than was needed by the farmers themselves. Some extra food was paid in taxes to the kings. These kings used their wealth to pay soldiers to protect the farmlands from raiders, to build glorious temples to keep the favor of the gods, and to organize law and order throughout their lands.

Above: Early bronze tools from about 2500 BC – a fishhook and a sickle for harvesting wheat.

Farming techniques
Throughout the thousands of years of Mesopotamian civilization, farming techniques changed little. Farmers were unwilling to try new agricultural methods when a failed crop could lead to famine and death. Fields were plowed, one furrow at a time, by oxen pulling wooden plows. Grain was sown by hand. Harvesting was back-breaking work, with workers cutting grain stems by hand using sharp knives or sickles.

Below: As farming tools and techniques became more efficient, farmers could grow more food. By about 3000 BC in Sumer, parts of wooden plows had been replaced by stronger bronze blades.

Above: A shepherd brings a goat kid to the royal palace of Sargon II of Assyria. Taxes were paid in agricultural goods by most farmers and herdsmen.

This relief shows a man using a shaduf, which was an irrigation tool. A bucket at the end of a long pole could be swiveled around to transfer water between canals.

Irrigation
The Euphrates and Tigris Rivers dominated Mesopotamia, providing essential water supplies for crops, animals, and people. When the rivers overflowed their banks, they deposited a rich layer of fertile silt on the surrounding farmland. The Mesopotamians were one of the first civilizations to develop systems of irrigation; during moderate floods, water was diverted into man-made channels next to the rivers and was stored in large dams. Then it was distributed to the fields through systems of aqueducts and canals as it was needed. Irrigation in Mesopotamia may have begun as long ago as the early 6th millennium BC.

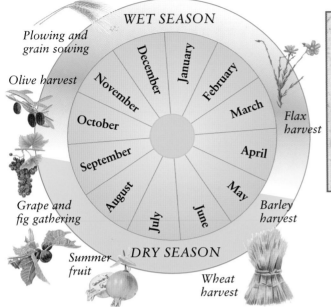

Plowing and grain sowing

WET SEASON

December
January
November
February
October
March
September
April
August
May
July
June

DRY SEASON

Olive harvest

Flax harvest

Barley harvest

Grape and fig gathering

Summer fruit

Wheat harvest

The agricultural calendar

Life for the farmers of Mesopotamia followed an annual cycle (above). In October the first rains came, preparing grain fields for plowing and sowing while olives were harvested. Throughout the wet season the crops grew; flax was harvested in March and grains a few weeks later. Throughout the dry season the fields were irrigated with water from the rivers while grapes, figs, and dates ripened in the summer sun. By the time these fruits were harvested and dried, the rains came, starting the cycle again.

FOOD IN MESOPOTAMIA

Meals in ancient Mesopotamia were luxurious compared to those of other peoples at the time. Grains were ground into flour and used to bake loaves of flat bread, or used to thicken soups. Vegetables, herbs, and spices were used to create rich soups and stews. Meat or fish was a luxury that most families only enjoyed from time to time, though nobles might eat meat every day. Fruit was eaten in large quantities, often as a dessert.

Agricultural products

Food from times of plenty was stored and preserved for times when food was scarce. Large pots were filled with fruits and buried in the cool ground. The tops were sealed with clay and wax to prevent air from entering and spoiling food. Milk was churned into butter or made into cheese. Fruits not eaten fresh were dried in the sun, then packed into jars.

Above: This section of a frieze, from around 2500 BC, shows people making butter from cows' milk.

Animals

Although sheep and goats (left) were the first animals to be domesticated, the Mesopotamians valued cattle more highly. The cylinder seal impression in green (above) shows a herd of cattle and a pair of cow barns. The bull (right) became a symbol of strength in religion, and it was often featured in sacrifices.

Ishtar in the Underworld

Ishtar, the goddess of love, was the most beautiful goddess of all. She was deeply in love with her husband Tammuz, a handsome shepherd. One day Tammuz was killed and taken to the land of the dead by Ishtar's enemy Ereshkigal, the queen of the Underworld.

Ishtar traveled to the Underworld to rescue Tammuz. When she arrived at the first gate she was met by Namtar, messenger of Ereshkigal, whose job was to collect the dead from the Earth.

"Before you pass this gate," said Namtar, "you must take off your crown." Ishtar did as she was told. They came to a second gate. "Before you pass this gate," said Namtar, "you must remove your earrings." Again, Ishtar obeyed the instruction. They passed through seven gates, and at each gate Ishtar was told to remove an item of jewelry or clothing. Finally she was completely naked.

The queen of the Underworld laughed. She had tricked Ishtar. Everyone was helpless in the Underworld if they were naked. Namtar sent sixty diseases to attack every part of Ishtar's body, and Ereshkigal threw her in prison.

Without the goddess of love, no crops would grow on Earth and no babies or young animals would be born. Ea, the god of rivers, realized what had happened. He created Asushu-Namir, a very beautiful man, and cast powerful magical spells to force Ereshkigal to obey instructions.

Asushu-Namir was sent to the Underworld. When Ereshkigal ordered him thrown into prison, Asushu-Namir uttered a magical spell. He ordered the queen of the Underworld to release her prisoner. As Ishtar walked back through each of the seven gates, she stopped to pick up her clothing and ornaments. When she reappeared on Earth she was as strong, beautiful, and as magnificent as ever. The crops started to flourish again, and the people worshiped Ishtar even more than before. But, although she was free, Ishtar had been unsuccessful in her quest to bring Tammuz back from the dead.

Clothing and Jewelry

Mesopotamian clothing and jewelry showed the differences between rich and poor, priests and secular people, and was designed for comfort and decoration. In the earliest periods, clothing was made from linen or from sheep or goats' wool. Around 1000 BC, the Mesopotamians started to grow cotton, which had been imported from India. Silk was a rare fabric which was imported from China and was very expensive. Wealthy people wore jewelry of gold, and colored and precious stones, but even the poorest could afford necklaces and bracelets of colored glass beads or brightly colored pottery.

Above: A reconstruction of the jewelry and ornate headdress of Pu-abi, a princess buried in Ur about 2600 BC.

Gold

Gold was used to make jewelry for the nobility. Most gold jewelry was made from gold nuggets found in streams. It was hammered, cut, or bent into shape, and intricate patterns could be embossed with tiny chisels and knives. Sumerian goldsmiths attached delicate gold decorations to larger pieces of jewelry with fish glue and copper hydroxide. When heated, this mixture gently fused the gold together without melting it.

A Sumerian necklace of beaten gold. The gold used in Mesopotamia was probably imported from around the Arabian Gulf, though some would have come from what is now Iran.

Above: A female face, originally part of a piece of furniture, shows the type of hairstyle and makeup typical of Assyria around 750 BC.

Left: Red carnelian and blue lapis lazuli, as seen in this outer necklace, were the most commonly used stones in Mesopotamian jewelry. The carnelian came from western India while the lapis lazuli was probably imported from the Hindu Kush.

Hairstyles

Carvings and paintings show that hairstyles were also used to differentiate between social classes. Peasants had simple cropped hairstyles that were practical for work in the fields. Noblemen had their hair carefully cut and shaped into curls. These styles were elegant but would have been impossible to maintain for a person who had to do hard physical work. Courtiers also wore makeup and used dyes to color their hair and eyebrows.

Below: In about 700 BC, an Elamite woman uses a spindle to spin woolen thread. Even the noblest women were expected to spin, weave, and sew.

Above: Two Assyrian noblemen of about 750 BC. The square-cut beards and long hair remained in fashion in northern Mesopotamia for centuries.

A servant fans the lady

Embroidered hem of cloak

Spindle

Women's work

Throughout Mesopotamia, women were expected to make the cloth and clothing for their families, and even rich noblewomen would spin and sew. The simple tools that Mesopotamian women used meant that it took at least 24 days to produce a piece of cloth about 9x12 feet in size. The cloth would then be cut and sewn into simple cloaks or tunics.

Right: Babylonian sandals from about 550 BC. All types of people wore similar styles of sandals, although peasants tended to wear sandals made of braided straw while nobles wore soft leather sandals.

SPECIAL ROYAL CLOTHING

King Zimri-Lim (1775-60 BC) of Mari wearing the ceremonial kilt worn by royalty on special occasions (left). These types of kilts were worn in Sumeria, but rarely elsewhere. It was believed that if the king made any mistake during religious ceremonies, or while supervising festivals, the gods might become angry and punish the city. The elaborate ceremonial kilt was a sign of this very important role that the king played.

NERGAL AND ERESHKIGAL

One day the king of the gods decided to hold a banquet. Ereshkigal, goddess of the land of the dead, could not travel to the king's palace, and the king could not travel to the land of the dead. So it was decided that Ereshkigal's messenger should collect Ereshkigal's share of the feast from the palace.

But when the messenger arrived, Nergal, the god of disease, did not rise to greet him. When Ereshkigal learned of this she was furious and told her messenger, "I have been insulted. Bring Nergal to me so that I may kill him." The messenger returned to the palace and invited Nergal to the land of the dead to feast with Ereshkigal.

But Nergal's father Ea, the god of rivers, suspected a trick. He told Nergal, "When she offers you bread, do not eat it, for it is the bread of death. When she offers you water, do not drink it, for it is the drink of death."

When Nergal arrived in the land of the dead he was offered food, but he would not eat it. Then he was offered water, but he would not drink it. He was also offered a chair to sit on and a bowl in which to wash his feet, and he refused both of these things. Then he was offered a beautiful cloak, which he accepted and put on. Ereshkigal was furious that Nergal had avoided her traps, because she had fallen in love with him and wanted to keep him in the Underworld. But Nergal escaped.

Ereshkigal demanded that the gods return him to her, or she threatened to raise all the dead so that they would outnumber the living. So Nergal was sent back to the Underworld, with fourteen demons sent by Ea to protect him. The demons guarded the gate against Ereshkigal's monsters while Nergal leapt at the goddess. He dragged Ereshkigal from the throne by her hair and threw her to the ground.

Ereshkigal then cried out, "Do not kill me! Be my husband and I will grant you authority in the vast world of the dead." Nergal then bent down and kissed the goddess saying, "What you have been seeking will now be yours." Ereshkigal realized how much she loved Nergal. Together they ruled the Underworld and gathered people to their kingdom.

Daily Life

Most people in ancient Mesopotamia were farmers or shepherds. Many citizens of the great southern Mesopotamian cities left their homes each morning to work in the fields surrounding each city. About one in ten people worked in more specialized jobs – they might be weavers, jewelers, butchers, or brickmakers. In the larger cities many people worked for the government or for the temples. They were able to read and write, and worked to keep records of taxes, enforce laws, or maintain public buildings.

This small stone carving of a married couple from Babylon shows them holding hands, a formal symbol of love.

The family

Throughout Mesopotamia, a family usually consisted of a married couple with their children, although other relatives might live in the same house or in a nearby house. Most children followed their parents to become farmers, potters, or bakers, although a rich person might pay for a gifted child to be properly educated. The children of nobles and priests were often trained as scribes, so they could enter a range of careers in government service or among temple staff.

This goblet was made from pure gold around 2500 BC. Noblemen drank fine wines at banquets, but wine goblets as valuable as this were reserved for monarchs.

This stone carving (c. 860 BC) shows scenes in the preparation of a meal: 1. A servant girl checks the storeroom for ingredients. 2. Women mix ingredients using whisks made from reeds. 3. Meat is butchered. 4. A baker checks his oven and its contents.

This Sumerian fisherman figure is from around 2600 BC. Great rivers and swamps provided plenty of fish for Sumerian meals.

Food habits

Most people in ancient Mesopotamia ate a basic diet of wheat or barley bread with dates, onions, peas, and lentils. Cheese made of sheep or goats' milk was common, but meat was rarely eaten except by the richest people. Wild animals were also caught and eaten, but they were rare in the densely populated areas of Mesopotamia. Most people drank beer, although wine was enjoyed by the wealthy.

Entertainment

Hundreds of Mesopotamian board games have been found by archaeologists, but we do not know the rules for these games. Other toys included model boats, animals, and soldier figures. Music was very important in richer households, and the wealthiest families owned lyres and other instruments decorated with gold and lapis lazuli.

Above: A board game with playing pieces made of shell, bone, and stone. Dating from about 2500 BC, the board was probably used for a popular race game.

Right: This model clay house from Hama dates from about 2500 BC. It shows the kind of houses that farmers and ordinary citizens lived in at the time.

Houses

All houses in ancient Mesopotamia were built of mud brick – blocks of mud mixed with straw and left out to dry in the sun. They consisted of just one or two rooms, although a barn for livestock might be attached.

Above: Toy animals mounted on wheels were very popular in Babylon and may have been played with by younger children.

Above: A reconstruction of a lyre from Ur from about 2500 BC.

Traveling

Most people did not travel very far, perhaps only to the next city, and they often walked. However merchants, nobles, and priests might travel hundreds of miles to visit other countries. Donkeys were used to carry packs, or sometimes for riding, while oxen pulled carts. Horses were used only by the wealthiest people.

Below: A family group from Babylon, about 750 BC, ride in a cart pulled by oxen. The spoked wheel was an important Babylonian invention, as it made carts much lighter and more practical.

THE EPIC OF ERRA

Erra was the warrior of the gods and the commander of the Sebitti, seven gods of war who marched at his side when he went into battle. There had been peace in Babylon for a long time, but the Sebitti began to cry loudly that they were growing bored and old with no more battles. Erra's weapons complained,

"We have become blunt, and rusty, and covered in spiders' webs, and we have almost forgotten how to fight! It is time for a war!"

Erra believed that Marduk had become a lazy ruler, allowing his people in Babylon to become too numerous and noisy, and he decided to begin a war in the city. But first he had to get Marduk out of the way.

"Your crown looks so battered and

dirty," he told Marduk. "It is not fit for a god who rules a city as beautiful as Babylon."

Erra persuaded Marduk to go in search of the skilled craftspeople who could restore his crown to its original golden brilliance. The craftspeople lived far from Babylon, and Marduk was reluctant to leave his temple, not knowing what would happen if he was not there to protect his people. So Erra offered to stay in his place and watch over Babylon while Marduk was away.

Marduk agreed and started on his journey. As soon as Marduk had left the city, Erra began to spread devastation – he set families against each other, creating conflict and wars. Shrines, temples, palaces, and houses were destroyed in the fighting, and many people were killed.

Finally Ishum intervened and pleaded with Erra to bring an end to the destruction. But Erra would only stop the wars if the other gods accepted his demand that they become his servants. They had no choice but to agree.

War and Weapons

Warfare was a common part of life in Sumeria and Babylonia. Cities fought each other for control of fertile fields or profitable trade routes. Raiders would fight to loot and plunder treasures and riches. Some rulers, such as the Assyrian kings, set out to conquer other lands and peoples to force them to pay taxation and tribute money. The history of the area is one of shifting alliances, rising and falling empires, and frequent rebellions.

Above: An Assyrian king on horseback, from about 700 BC, shoots an arrow during a hunt. The mounted archer was a formidable opponent on the battlefield.

Above: This gold dagger sheath from Byblos was made about 1900 BC. It is decorated with a hunting scene.

Left: An Assyrian warrior of about 750 BC carries a spear and shield, and wears a coat of iron mail for protection.

Professional soldiers

Professional fighters used special weapons and armor that distinguished them from ordinary citizens going to fight. Hours of training and great strength were needed to use the large shields, powerful bows, and long spears. Armor – made of bronze plates or iron-studded leather – was expensive and heavy, so only a few men wore it. These professional soldiers were well paid by kings and other rulers, and sometimes they could even set themselves up as rulers over cities.

Below: Assyrians wore bronze armor like this when they went to battle.

War strategies

The earliest battles in Babylonia and Sumeria were fought between citizens of neighboring cities. Fighters formed a solid phalanx and advanced, walking towards the enemy. Victory was usually achieved through brute force and sheer numbers. By about 2000 BC most armies had an elite force of professional soldiers. They were trained to use more specialized tactics and weapons, as well as chariots. Many wars, however, were decided by city sieges, and losers were often forced to pay taxes to the winner. Sometimes the losers were sold as slaves or even slaughtered, and their property was taken from them.

Above: This pure gold helmet was made in Ur around 2,500 BC for ceremonial purposes. Gold is too soft to offer much protection in battle. Holes around the helmet's edges allowed leather padding to be attached.

Above: This carving from Lagash (about 2450 BC) shows helmeted warriors with shields locked together. They formed a solid, protective wall with their spears protruding. This formation was known as a phalanx.

Right: A Syrian man using a slingshot (850 BC). These could be deadly weapons and were often used in battle.

Weapons

Most weapons used in warfare were identical to those used by hunters, or by shepherds guarding their flocks. Most men would go to war carrying their household weapons with them; only a few professionals were trained to use chariots or other weapons especially for war.

Below: A dagger of a type common around 1500 BC.

Left: War chariots and soldiers from Ur, about 2500 BC. The chariots were pulled by asses and could travel little further than a man could run, but they proved to be effective mobile fighting platforms in several battles.

ETANA AND THE EAGLE

When the city of Kish was still very young, the gods Enlil and Ishtar decided to find it a king. They chose the wise shepherd Etana. For many years Etana ruled well, but as he grew old he worried that he did not have a son to be the king of Kish after him. Etana prayed to Shamash, the sun god and god of justice, asking for a son. Shamash replied, "Take to the road and reach the mountain and ask an eagle to bring you the herb of birth from the home of Anu."

After a long journey, Etana reached the mountain and found a giant eagle lying in a ditch with his wings broken. Unknown to Etana, the eagle had been cursed by Shamash for eating the children of a serpent that belonged to the sun god.

Etana asked the eagle to help him find the herb of birth. The eagle replied that he would take Etana to the herb, if Etana would bring him food to keep him strong while his wings

healed. After Etana had brought food to the eagle for several months, the eagle recovered his strength and was able to fly again. Etana climbed onto the eagle's back and they soared up into the sky toward the home of Anu. But as the eagle flew higher, Etana grew frightened and cried out, "My friend, I can climb no higher. Stop!" And so the eagle returned him to the ground. For several nights, Etana dreamed about flying high into the sky and of having a son, and finally he decided to try again. This time he was not afraid as the eagle ascended to the heavens, and together they succeeded in finding the precious herb of birth that would give Etana a son and heir to the kingdom. Etana returned to his city, and soon afterward he had a son named Balih, who became the king of Kish after Etana died.

Kings and Cities

Cities were the basis of all government in Mesopotamia. Each city governed the surrounding farmland and local villages. Early cities were ruled by a council of elders, men from the richest or oldest families. Later, the men who commanded the army or the temple came to dominate the councils, and by about 2600 BC these men were calling themselves kings. The kings claimed to rule because they had been chosen by the gods, but they still had to leave some decisions to the councils. By 1500 BC most kings ruled more than one city. They were enormously powerful and could do almost anything they liked; the local elders or governors were allowed to decide only local matters.

King Hammurabi, founder of the Old Babylonian empire, is shown in this small statuette praying to a god. The figure is of bronze, but the face and hands are covered in gold.

Above: A relief of the hero Gilgamesh, who was King of Uruk in about 2000 BC. Here he is taming a lion cub. Gilgamesh was the center of many stories. The most famous of these were written down in the Epic of Gilgamesh, *which has survived to the present day. It portrays him as a king who leads his people successfully but tries to become immortal and ends up facing death alone.*

Above: Sargon of Akkad, who ruled from about 2334 BC to 2279 BC. He was the first monarch to unite a great empire in Mesopotamia.

Left: The King List, written about 2000 BC in Sumer, claims to list rulers of the various cities from about 3000 BC onward.

Below: King Sargon II of Assyria, who ruled from 721 to 705 BC, conquered lands as far as the borders of Egypt.

Below: Slaves working on the construction of Sennacherib's palace in Nineveh.

The Assyrian kings

The city of Nineveh was the center of the Assyrian empire. The Assyrians were masters of warfare, and they used fast chariots to outflank enemies in the battlefield and powerful siege engines to smash city walls. By 660 BC the Assyrian empire covered all of Mesopotamia as well as parts of Egypt and Palestine. In 612 BC, Nineveh was conquered by a coalition of Babylon and northern barbarians and was utterly destroyed.

Left: The Hanging Gardens of Babylon were listed as one of the Seven Wonders of the World. They were built on terraces in the royal palace and were irrigated by water pumped from the Euphrates River.

Babylon

Babylon had already been a prosperous city for many generations when, about 1792 BC, King Hammurabi united the many cities of Sumer and Akkad, making Babylon the largest and wealthiest city in the world. In 1595 BC Babylon was destroyed by King Murshili of the Hittites. By 1390 BC the city had been rebuilt and was a major religious center. But Babylon was controlled by foreign rulers until Nabopolassar led it to independence in about 625 BC. Babylon was rebuilt in spectacular style and became again the mightiest city in the world. However, in 539 BC the Persians conquered Babylon, and it soon became a small provincial city. By about AD 75 Babylon was totally abandoned.

The Ishtar Gate was the main northern entrance to the city of Babylon.

MAP OF BABYLON
1 – Euphrates River
2 – Ishtar Gate
3 – Tower of Babel
4 – Marduk's Temple
5 – Ramparts

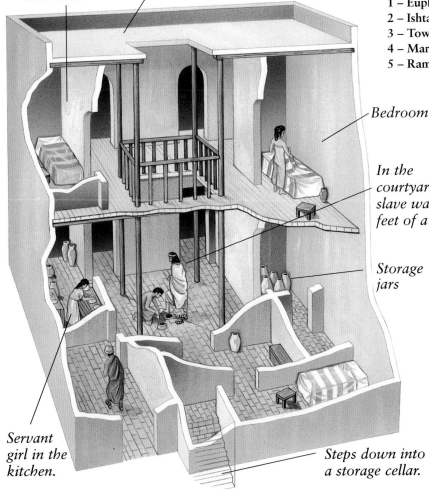

Flat roofs were used for sleeping on during hot seasons.

Bedroom

Bedroom

In the courtyard, a slave washes the feet of a visitor.

Storage jars

Servant girl in the kitchen.

Steps down into a storage cellar.

Houses

Mesopotamian houses were built of mud brick with wooden posts and beams. There were no windows looking out onto the streets, only a small doorway which could be locked to protect the house from intruders. Light entered the house through a courtyard at the center, from which doors led to the various rooms. Wealthier families had an entire house such as this to themselves, but poorer families would have occupied one or two rooms per family.

MARDUK AND NABU

Once every year, the gods all gathered together in Upshukina, the palace of fate. There they discussed the destinies of men and women and argued about who should live and who should die, which people should be rich and which people should be poor. The final decisions were made by Marduk, king of the gods, but all the gods and goddesses took part in the discussion and put forward their arguments and opinions.

When Marduk reached his decisions, he whispered them to his son Nabu who carefully wrote the fate of each person down on his special clay tablet. When the time was right, Nabu checked the writing on his tablets to make sure of Marduk's orders. He then summoned the appropriate god, goddess, or demon, who was sent to Earth to carry out Marduk's instructions. Sin, the moon god, always stood close to Marduk during the

discussions and sometimes he overheard Marduk's decisions or caught a glimpse of what Nabu was writing. Then Sin would send his messenger Zaqar to Earth to warn people of the fate in store for them. Zaqar moved through the night and whispered to people in their dreams. However, people did not always hear him correctly and sometimes misunderstood the voices in their dreams.

One year, Nabu came down from the palace of Marduk with his wife, Tashmetum. They lived on Earth for some time in the city of Borsippa. There Nabu and Tashmetum taught people how to read and write so that they could keep a record of the lives and destinies of men and women, just as Nabu wrote his own records of Marduk's instructions. Nabu and Tashmetum eventually returned to the heavens, but people have continued teaching each other how to read and write ever since.

Written Language

The invention of writing was a key development in the history of civilization. For the first time it was possible to pass information from one person to another without actually speaking to them. Instead, a messenger could carry the writing, or the writing could be left for somebody to find. Some of the earliest forms of writing come from the city of Uruk in Sumer and date to about 3100 BC. Pictures were used to represent objects, while abstract marks indicated numbers. Later, triangular-shaped reeds were used to make marks called cuneiform (meaning "wedge-shaped") in moist clay tablets. Cuneiform writing was used for about 3,000 years and became a sophisticated method of writing dozens of different languages.

Stones and Clay

Most writing was done on wet clay tablets. If the writing was only temporary, the tablet could be moistened again and wiped clean, but if the information was meant to be permanent the tablet would be baked hard in the sun. Some very important texts were carved on stone. These were often displayed in public places so that everyone could have access to the information contained in the writing.

Above: The great law stone of King Hammurabi, from about 1780 BC. The writing sets out the punishments for various crimes and would have stood in the law courts to ensure that everyone received the same treatment.

Right: A cylinder seal of about 1750 BC, and the impression it makes. The seals were rolled in wet clay to authenticate documents or accounts. This one is typical in showing a hero and a god, together with the name and rank of the person who owns it.

This cone originally decorated a wall. The writing thanks the god Ningir-su for settling a dispute.

Right: An early cuneiform text from about 2900 BC. Words and numbers that relate to each other are put together in boxes, but there is no formal order to the words.

Below: Beautifully decorated with symbols and pictures sacred to the gods – for instance the crescent moon of Ishtar – this stone was set up to mark the boundary between separate plots of land.

Boundary Markers

A piece of writing could be read by anyone, even if they did not know who had written the text or why. This made the skill very useful for marking boundaries. The edges of farmland, districts, and even kingdoms were marked by stone and clay tablets that could be read and understood by travelers.

Dedicatory Texts

When construction work began on important buildings, such as palaces or temples, the help of the gods was invoked. Small carvings of gods, and tablets requesting their protection, were often placed among the foundations.

Left: This small carving of a god holds a "nail" that secured a dedicatory text in a building's foundations.

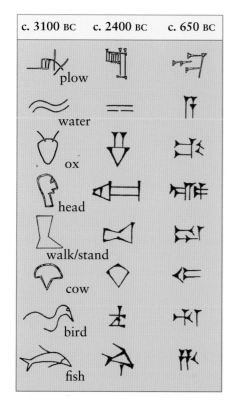

Right: This small tablet is carved with script asking for the blessings of the gods to fall upon a building.

Above: A map drawn in about 700 BC. The valley of the Euphrates River is shown within the large circle, with smaller circles representing towns. The markings outside the circle represent legendary lands and imaginary places.

Right: A small figure carrying a basket. The text around the base indicates the object placed in the basket.

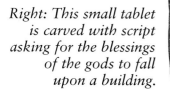

Left: Cuneiform markings changed over time. Early pictures were formalized by about 2400 BC, and by 650 BC they were so stylized it was difficult to see their link to the original picture.

Right: Two scribes record a list of produce from a farm on a wall carving from Nineveh about 630 BC. The nearest scribe holds a clay tablet and reed marker, the other uses a pen and roll of paper. By this date cuneiform writing was considered an old-fashioned type of writing, used only for formal government accounts.

Craftspeople and Trade

The ancient Mesopotamians traded among themselves, and also with people living hundreds of miles away. Goods that could not be found in Mesopotamia were brought in from elsewhere. Timber was imported to north and south Mesopotamia from the mountains, gold was brought from the Arabian Gulf, ivory came from Egypt, cinnamon and myrrh from Somalia, olive oil from the Mediterranean, and ebony from India. Goods were either swapped for other items, including grain and pottery, or paid for with silver.

Above: Enameled bricks were fired at high temperatures and used to decorate important buildings.

Skilled craftspeople

As the populations of the great cities grew, craftspeople became more skilled. Individuals started specializing in producing one type of object, which they then traded for other things they needed. Skilled potters, for instance, made ceramics which they swapped for fruit from farmers, metal tools from metalsmiths, and bread from bakers. Each city had a whole community of potters, bakers, launderers, butchers, builders, and carpenters within its walls. Some cities specialized in particular crafts and traded with neighboring cities for other items. Tilmun, for instance, specialized in copper goods.

Below: A reconstructed copper-smelting furnace from around 1250 BC.

Above: A decorated pottery beaker from about 4000 BC. Pottery-making was among the first of the specialized crafts to develop.

Above: This tiny jug is decorated with inlaid colored pottery.

A bronze rein ring, with a gilded horse for decoration, used in Ur about 2600 BC.

Below: Delicate cups were made by hammering sheet gold into shape. This cup was made in Ur around 1600 BC.

Smelting metal

Gold is sometimes found in pure nuggets, but other metals have to be smelted from rock ores. To obtain copper, Mesopotamians packed crushed copper ore and charcoal into a furnace. Bellows fanned the flames to create high temperatures. When the plug was removed the molten rock flowed off, leaving pure copper in the base of the furnace.

Trade routes of the 2nd millennium BC

Above: Main trade routes of about 2000 BC are shown in red. These linked various cities of the Near East, following valleys and open plains where traveling was easiest.

Weights and Measures

The methods used by Mesopotamians to weigh and measure goods were based on familiar natural objects. Lengths were commonly measured in "hands" or "arms," while weights were explained in terms of grains of wheat. From about 2500 BC merchants had metal or stone weights, which they used to ensure that quantities of goods were as heavy as the seller claimed.

Above: This relief statue shows a camel loaded with goods being led through the desert. Camels were first tamed around 1700 BC.

Left: A modern reconstruction of a sled seat that would have been pulled by two oxen. Such sleds were used for transporting goods and people across flat ground.

Left: A pair of Assyrian bronze weights shaped as lions.

Left: This stone weight in the shape of a duck is carved with an inscription guaranteeing its precise weight in the name of Shulgi, moon goddess of Ur.

In ancient Mesopotamia gold or silver coins were not stamped with a design to guarantee their weight, so precious metals had to be weighed for each business transaction.

TRADING WITHOUT MONEY

By about 4000 BC, Mesopotamians were using simple clay shapes to record business deals (below). The shapes of wheat grains or rolls of cloth may have been used to show how many goods were owed by one person to another. Later, business deals were written on clay tablets so that both the buyer and seller had records of which goods had been exchanged.

INDEX